THE ONLY REASON FOR TIME

FIONA MOORE

HAPPENSTANCE

ISBN 978-1-905939-90-9

Acknowledgements:

Thanks to editors of the following magazines in which some of these poems, or versions of them, first appeared: *The Bow-Wow Shop, Brittle Star, Magma, Orbis, Poetry London, The Rialto, The SHOp, Smiths Knoll, Under the Radar.*

Printed by The Dolphin Press
www.dolphinpress.co.uk

Published in 2013 by Happen*Stance,*
21 Hatton Green, Glenrothes, Fife KY7 4SD
nell@happenstancepress.com
www.happenstancepress.com

Orders:
Individual pamphlets £4.00 (includes UK P&P).
Please make cheques payable to Helena Nelson
or order through PayPal in the website shop.

CONTENTS

To Graham

POSTCARD

Three days, and already I could write
a dissertation on the fastenings of gates:

the counterintuitive, industry standard
grey metal latch, to be clanged backwards;

the bolt with a spring that's always too strong;
the soft warmth of an old chain, brown stream

through fingers, binding the post with a hook;
the double gate's hard-edged central loop

with its guillotine rise/drop; and the frayed
Gordian knot of orange nylon twine, avoided

by climbing at the hinge end. Each one
a puzzle, each to be handled and worked on,

each gate lifted or pulled, before I pass
from the last room of sheep or meadow flowers—

below hills that move up, and down, and up
as if walking their own walk—

to the next. With love.

GETTING UP AT SIX

Your feet step down each stair
and then, as I hear you gather one by one
the things you heaped on the table late last night,
I wonder, what does it feel like to be you
as you stand there, filling the small room,
your long reach when you pocket the clatter of change,
your knuckles grazing the smooth lining, still cool;
to be you as you slide the lozenge phone into your jacket,
as your hand engulfs the thistlehead of keys
(what are they all for?) the wallet, the rail-pass,
and you straighten your spine, your shoulders, balanced . . .

The gate screeches when you lift the cold bar of the latch
and I wonder, half asleep in the circle
of your warmth, what does it feel like to be you,
getting up at six
to be conveyed by train, by tube, by train, by plane . . .
As you lope off to the station,
phone bumping against your chest,
what do your hands remember?

THE SHIRT

I didn't find it for months, your shirt
bundled into a corner in the airing cupboard.
I shook it out. It had been cut
with long cuts, all the way up the sleeves
and up the front, so it looked like a plan
of something about to be put together.
They must have had to work so fast to
save you there was no time to unbutton it.
An office shirt, because that's where
it happened. The thin stripes slashed through—
terrifying, unprecedented—a reminder
of everything I wanted to forget.
I'd washed it afterwards, not knowing what to do
with it, or that in three weeks the same thing
would happen to another shirt, a favourite,
dull cotton whose thick weave made it look
as if all the pink shell-grains of sand
had come together on one beach,
a shirt for a gentle hug; and from then on,
nothing happened that we would forget.

IOIOIOIOIO...

Your death works in binary mode
on/off, forget/remember—
a cold code to decipher,
too late for us.

Your death kills me a thousand times,
the tyranny of repetition—
you/me, here/there.
Zero/one.

HUNGER

One way to dispose of a corpse is to eat it.

The skeleton lies on my plate, fish-perfect, scavenger food.
It reminds me of the last time we ate mackerel together.

Necrophagy. Even the dictionary half-shuns the word.
Somewhere between perversion and religion there must be
a space for this confusion of eating and death.

After your funeral I was hungry, for the first time in weeks.
Beer, sandwiches, tea and cake: death's nursery food. That
was months ago. Now I'm full of mackerel, the complete
feeling that comes from eating a whole creature.

Necrophagy. Even the dictionary half-shuns the word.
Somewhere between perversion and religion there must be
a space for this confusion of eating and death.

The skeleton lies on my plate, fish-perfect, scavenger food.
It reminds me of the last time we ate mackerel together.

One way to dispose of a corpse is to eat it.

EDEN

(by the River Narew, near Różan, north-east Poland, 1986)

Where nature spewed out immaculate crowds
of baby frogs like a chemical reaction,
grass-green, brown, leaping all over the meadow.

Where each butterfly was new as an invention,
each beetle an exact blueprint, and damselflies
swarmed in storm-clouds above the tangled river

and night was the colour of the damselflies,
starlit perfection, the frogs' echo chamber,
then a swish of rain and the warm smell of earth.

Where storks balanced the messy bar of their nests
on telegraph poles and barn roofs, and the sun
swung higher each day, as if it would forever.

Where all horizons were limitlessly flat,
stands of pine forest alternating with rye—
and the rye field I walked into one day, led by a path

of trodden stalks, to the secret square brimming
with opium poppies, white/purple bleed of petals,
seedpods about to swell, the shock of intention.

THE NUMBERS

The numbers. Etched in faded indigo: maybe half a dozen,
small and precise.
On close inspection, blurred as if the skin had puckered them
rather than they the skin. The lower arm's soft skin,
another vein or blotch of age.

Occasionally—
just as one might board the same tram as usual, but arrive
somewhere unexpected—
occasionally it would happen. In random settings and
conversations
someone would push up a sleeve and show me
the numbers. Always casually,
and as a matter of fact.

OVERWINTER

This is midwinter's longest day
that absorbs its own silence of waiting.
Nothing moves through the air
and gravity seems a miracle, the earth's grip
made of so much more than frost.
Instead the ground-mist floats the trees
whose outlines are all gesture,
each miming the wait differently.
Nothing will happen for a while, nothing—
and I need such certainty: to become
embedded deep within this season
when dark overplaits the day's pale strand.
Change may come while nothing seems to change.
I know it will take a long time.

TO THE MOON I: NEW YEAR'S EVE

Full moon, casket of wishes, neat-lidded
moon, heavenframed—
ten thousand ghosts are furled inside your circle.

Moon, I will post LOVE, a midnight blue word
across your face
to roll with you slowly in three dimensions,

turned towards earth and inextricable
from a sky deep
enough to hold all dreams. Looked at for as long

as I look at you, LOVE will soon become
meaningless. So
I will formalise the losing of hope:

for your course, moon, is solitary, you journey
without trading,
though not without leading astray. Zone me

into your treeless, pale desolation
O moon, and let
your distance wane my thought by its proportions.

'O THAT INSISTENT THOUGHT'

—George Seferis

The river's surface had many variables:
downstream flow, tides, weather and unknown. The house
reflected it on white ceilings, to be read
like the palm of a hand whose fortune kept changing.
Stacked up against a cardboard factory
the narrow rooms held a riverine smell, and old
sounds: ripples slapping on wooden piles,
machinery next door, recycling.

One night a mouse ran and ran in the attic
until we trapped her under a cardboard box
and left her on the quay in the dark, to act out
the mind that concentrates on one thing and
gnaws at it, eating its own page into lace.
By dawn the box had a hole, facing deep
water as the mouse would have—stopped
on the edge of something immense.

OUTSIDE GRAMSCI'S HOUSE

The two of us, smiling at the learned young curator
who'd offered to take our picture. Behind us is the sign
House of Antonio Gramsci, and the front door, open
into a dark interior. Our shoulders are touching,
we are layered against the cold, and you're holding a package,
your hero on a red t-shirt. A vein ridges your hand.

One look and I'm with you, standing on the wet pavement
full of a shared hour spent looking and reading—
his hard life, long imprisonment and early death—
with you on our journey to get there, steep angled terraces
blazing black and green under white sun, the almond blossom
luminous.

I didn't keep the t-shirt
but now I see it in your hand, I wish I had.

TO THE MOON 2: LATE FEBRUARY

Moon, white-gowned eroticist, consumer
of our desires—
look how the world has slowly stripped for you

down to this pre-spring starkness: trees, undergrowth,
blank pavements and
my usual despair, worn out by night after

long dark night of nothing. Not much awake
at this cold hour
except foxes and a few uncurtained

lovers dressed in your steady light. But now,
moon, specialist
in our madness and midnight practices,

now I want to bare all for you, if only
so something must
happen. Reflect me back to myself: rare as

you are, bald as an unearthed Trojan helmet
and as intact,
as necessarily flawed, and silent.

'THE ONLY REASON FOR TIME IS SO THAT EVERYTHING DOESN'T HAPPEN AT ONCE'

—Albert Einstein

I will get language where I can,
I will recover you from time that is not
linear, as it seemed. You went out
through it like a door and will come back in
before you left, and intact:
what could be more ordinary
than this, or easier to say?
You, wearing clothes I've kept,
the Aran jersey of our first kiss, folded
to two dimensions, collapsing time
from its fourth: time, our sealant
in the parallel, never-to-meet,
where I live, you rot, and your jersey
holds me differently, loose, undyed.

TRULY

Rosslare on an early morning
    was grey with our lack of sleep
when we tumbled
    into a new country

then Ireland woke us
    a smell of green
and suddenly round a bend
    aslant in the ditch

canary yellow a car
    the doors wings
and by it gathered
    five nuns

like pints of stout
    just poured
in dialogue with a man
    mud on his boots

the sight vanished
    quick as this line   it was true
as I'm here now
    remembering it for you

ON DUNWICH BEACH

The brown sea raids the shore, where you lie not far
inland. I crouch on wet shingle, undressing for you.

I plunge in, slipping where the ground falls away,
gasping at the icy cold: now I'm swimming for you

though you'd never have swum in this, and I know it
but raise my head with the swell, searching for you.

Waves rock the pale horizon. I could swim on
until my heart falters and I'm dying for you

but I'd never find you. The water's embrace jolts,
heaves, lulls me . . . I kick hard, breathing for you

through strands of hair . . . The drab land calls, the sea
spits me out—numb, dripping salt, living for you.

NOTHING

The dark never changes, the dark stays dark,
the same things come out of it that always came:
  nothing + nothing is an answer.
The O of the eye, the sun, the ocean, stopped
by doors and ceilings and windows of earth:
  nothing + nothing is an answer.
The bejewelled din, heart of the storm,
an arm in a sleeve, a face clothed in blood:
red is old and a city like silence,
  nothing + nothing is an answer.
Night floods the day as water the sky,
the O of the cave, the whirlpool, the wormhole:
nothing + nothing is nothing, is all,
  nothing + nothing is an answer.

TO THE MOON 3: AUTUMN EQUINOX

O moon, pale opposite of a shadow—so
unexpected
at the shore's vanishing point, in balance

with the sun gone down. First inkling: now you
strengthen and rise
full neon, prototype of a mood, over

the sea into violet sky. Your trail runs
faint on blueish
water, but here on the darkening sand

it ripples in salt pools, a long finger
that beckons me.
When I come near, you retreat to a place

beyond understanding, where I can't follow.
Moon, here's a heart
in the sand—and over there a lantern, launched

straight for you, a circle of orange flame
soaring towards
destruction: the higher, the more complete.

BULLOCKS—

here, by this fence
sheltering under the trees,
a paint chart of browns—
startled, they look up,
jostle, and
they're away!
Down the hill, the green
straight, at a gallop—
all bunched up
shouldering each other,
muddy rumps rocking
up/down, hooves
thundering, rope-tails
flying . . . oh, the rain
roars for them
and the trees too—
the dark one has it
by a head from the roan
and the skewbald—
they're making such time
until they all loosen,
slow, fan out, gentle
themselves into a walk
as if they know exactly
when they've passed
their finishing line.

THE DISTAL POINT

We stand at the point of greatest change—
the distal point, a shingle spit
at the end of the longshore drift.
Here the waves curve
and spill, lacing across each other,
forming a landscape that moves
leached of colour.

No-one who stands here can see
down the length
of the wind's fetch
and only the gulls measure
the shape of the swell
as they swing high
on the fulls, low in the swales

and no-one has stood here before
where each accretion
becomes an erosion
from the diagonal swash
and straight backwash, the waves'
refraction and landfall.
No-one will stand here again.

SINK DRAIN

It's as much a place
as a thing—a space,
or rather a star
in space, iron star,
utilitarian
mid-20th-century
war decoration.
Six discoloured spokes
wheeling outwards
from a hollow circle
and ringed by stainless steel.

As much a symbol
as a place. The Order
of the Kitchen Sink:
for years of hard labour spent
digging out potato peel
and grains of left-over rice,
bent over the black hole
where we'll all end—space,
gut hole, wormhole,
place or non-place.

WHAT KIND OF SOUND CROWDS MAKE

The tube bursts out of its tunnel
into the wider cylinder of the station. People filter
from tube to platform, platform to tube. The doors

slam: but one set has trapped
a boy—his neck clamped in the rubberised edges,
double guillotine, and the nearby crowd says

oh, a collective moan of shock.
He's about ten, stuck, head inside the train, body
outside, between two worlds, snagging both of them.

The doors relax—not enough—and thud
closed again with what seems, against his neck, brutal force
as more people say *OH*, with protest in it this time,

and some try to pull the doors
apart, but it happens again, and a huge *OH* goes up
and shouts pass down the platform to the driver's end.

The boy stays still, silent. *OH*
fourth time—disbelief—then the doors open. He stumbles
backwards into people's arms, his face red and blank.

The sounds echo now, the *oh*s—
how spontaneous each one was and how exact
in its timing, and in the graded emotion, as if this

is the kind of sound crowds make
at executions of the surely innocent, when even
the expected, the moment of death, must be a shock.

THIRD DAY OF FOG

Hard to think about infinity
in a fog. Easier when the view
runs over a jigsaw of green fields
to the Atlantic, just a small
width visible between headlands
before it stretches forever
and shines like a gold path
at sunset. None of that
today, though fog does make
these colours brighter—
Narcissus wouldn't be ashamed
to view himself in puddles,
framed as he'd be by the flaming
orange, purple and fuchsia red
of an Irish hedge. He'd get a shock
when it all dulled in the mud.
What would you think of me
now? We must have kissed
within five miles of here.
The silence is dense enough
to allow room for voices,
and the fog presses close a smell
of damp grass and manure:
in itself, fog is
the very substance of a ghost.

AFTER FIVE YEARS

You would carry in dust on your feet
if you came back now: from as far away
as this thought, out of the first twilight
long enough to feel like spring.

Traveller from an antique land,
orbiter of legend and distant stars,

here you'd be: dazed by the earth, its green
perfection of circumstance,
the multiplicity of events and things,
what's new and what's stayed the same—

your feet winged by that strange dust.

TO THE READER

You are the fire around which your ghosts are talking.

They hand a segmented fruit, one to the next, to share,
and smoke a pipe. They discuss how the colour of ghosts
can only be seen when there is a thickness

of several at once; no transparent material is
transparent. They have passed you in streets, ordinary
or invisible, and their thoughts are graffiti

on all your vanished walls. Now they are gathered
at cold, indeterminate ground, wrapped in their own mist.
From time to time one of them reaches for more

wood, and throws it on the fire. Your flames leap up.